Grade 2

Scott Foresman

Decodable
Readers 1-15
Volume 1

PEARSON

Scott
Foresman

Editorial Offices: Glenview, Illinois • Parsippany, New Jersey
New York, New York
Sales Offices: Needham, Massachusetts • Duluth, Georgia • Glenview,
Illinois • Coppell, Texas • Sacramento, California • Mesa, Arizona

Contents

UNIT 3

Gus

Written by Harriet Yi
Illustrated by Josh Bermann

Phonics Skills

Short Vowels CVC, CVCC					Consonants -ck, -ng, -nk
has	Ken	his	got	pup	back
back	pet	six	job	Gus	quick
can	bell	big	not	fun	rang
fast	tell	quick	long	run	long
rang	let	did	lot	jump	bunk
nap	well	will	fond	tug	lick
mat	red	lick		bunk	
pat	bed			hug	
hand					

Ken has a pet pup.
Gus is his pup.
Ken was six
when he got Gus.

Gus was not big back then.
Gus got big quick.
Gus is as big as Ken.

Gus is fun.
Gus can run and jump.
Gus is fast.

Gus can tug on his bell.
It can tell Ken to let Gus out.
When the bell rang,
Ken did his job well.

At the end of his long day,
Gus will nap on his mat.
His mat is red.
It is under a bunk bed.

Ken can pat Gus on the head.
Gus will lick Ken on his hand.
Ken and Gus have fun together.

Ken will hug and pet
Gus a lot.
Ken is fond of
his big pup.

Ike and Ace

Written by Harry Doyle
Illustrated by Dan Vick

Phonics Skills

Long Vowels CVCe				c/s/, g/j/, s/s/	
age	mice	poke	cute	has	mice
make	nice	nose		is	nice
safe	fine	rose		age	cage
cage	Ike	home		Ace	wise
Ace	wise			his	nose
game	quite			rose	race
ate	bite			face	
race	life				
face					
made					

Tess has pet mice.
It is good at her age.
The mice make a home in
a nice, safe cage.

Tess will add fine mice beds for
Ike and for Ace.
Tess has a lid.
Tess is quite wise.

Tess can see her mice.
Ike can poke up his nose.
Ace can play a game.

Tess will put fine food
in their red pan.
Ike and Ace rose up
and ate every bite.

13

Ike is big and can not sit up.
Ace is small and cute.

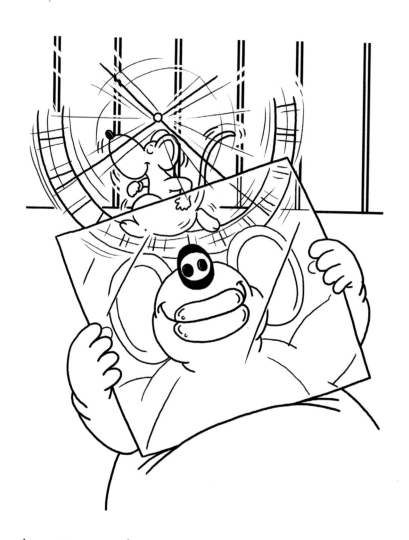

Ace is quick.
Ace can run in a race.
Ike can sit still
and make a face.

Ike and Ace have a fine life.
What luck for mice!
Tess has made a safe
home for Ike and Ace.

16

On Stage

Written by Amy Thornton
Illustrated by Kim Grant

Phonics Skill
Consonant Blends

and	stop	plan	glad	stage	strong	prop
black	mask	strap	act	skit	ask	next

The sun is not out.
It is not hot.
It is wet.
What a sad day!

18

Max and Mel stop
and make a plan.
They will make
Mom and Dad glad!

Max can make a stage.
It is wide and strong.
Mel can make a prop.
She will put the prop on stage.

20

Mel has a wig.
The wig is black.
Max has a mask.
He will strap it on.

They will act in a fun skit.
Mel can ask Mom and Dad
to sit in front of the stage.

Mel will sing a song.
Max will tell a joke.
Mom has fun.
Dad can laugh a lot.

Max and Mel are a big hit!
Next time the sun is not out,
they will act again.

Clive's Big Box

Written by Paula Alvarez
Illustrated by Barbra Johnson

Phonics Skill
Adding -s, -ed, -ing

dropped	lifting	makes	grabbed	yelled
lifted	wiped	smiling	smiled	added
rested				

Cam Clam dropped in
to see Clive Crab.
Clive makes his home
in an odd hole in a nice pond.

26

"Cam," said Clive,
"I am glad you came.
Can I get help
lifting this big box?"

"Lifting it will not be bad,"
Cam said with pride.
"I lift my home every day.
It makes me quite strong."

Cam bent down
and grabbed Clive's box.
Clive bent down
and grabbed his box.

"Lift on three," yelled Clive.
"One, two, three!"
Cam and Clive lifted at the same time.
Up came Clive's big box.

Clive and Cam set the box
on Clive's bed.
Clive wiped his face.
"Good job," Clive said, smiling.

Cam smiled back at Clive.
"Now we can rest," Cam added.
Clive and Cam sat and rested
in Clive's snug hole.

Will the Whale

Written by Allison Fisher
Illustrated by Brian Gilbert

Phonics Skill
Consonant Digraphs ch, tch, sh, th, wh

white	whale	fish	splashing	with
then	splash	when	this	ship(s)
shrimp	that	match		

Let me tell a tale
about Will the white whale.
Will is as big as a bus,
but he is quite nice.

34

Will is not a fish,
but he swims like one.
He likes swimming on his
back and splashing with his fin.

Will likes jumping up.
Then he makes a huge splash.
Will has fun gliding
on the wide waves.

When the wind
stopped and this ship got
stuck, Will helped.
Will pulled it to the dock.

Sid the Shrimp is
Will's best friend.
Big Will hides little Sid from
big hunting fish.

38

Will got a friend that
is a fine match.
His friend's name is El.
Will is glad that he met El.

Will and El splash
side by side.
They wave to ships
that pass them.

A Trip to the Farm

Written by Andrea Erwin
Illustrated by Steve Combs

Phonics Skills

R-controlled ar, or, ore			Syllables VCCV
Darling's	farm	before	Patrick
far	more	barn	Darling's
horses	Darling	porch	Darling
hard	chores	part	kitten
sore	arm	dark	rabbits

Patrick went to Jon Darling's farm.
Patrick had not gone
to this farm before.
"Is it far?" Patrick asked.
"Not much more," Mom said.

Patrick spotted Jon's farm.
"His farm has a big red barn!"
Patrick yelled.
"Are there horses, mules, and pigs?"
His mom grinned.

Jon Darling sat on his porch
with his kitten.
Patrick jumped out.
Patrick ran up to Jon.

"Are you set to work hard?"
Jon asked.
"We do chores on this farm."
Patrick will do his part
as well as he can.

Patrick swept pens.
Patrick fed chicks and rabbits.
Jon fixed his barn.

Jon Darling stretched his sore back
and patted Patrick's arm.
"You did a nice job," Jon said.

When it got dark,
Patrick went home.
"That was fun!" Patrick said.

Jem Wasn't Happy

Written by Stephen Lewis
Illustrated by Ann Mitcham

Phonics Skill

Contractions n't, 's, 'll, 'm

didn't	I'm	isn't	let's	it'll

Jem liked her food.
Jem liked her yard.
Jem liked her bones
and fun things.

50

But Jem didn't look glad.
Jem moped in the yard.
Jem is not well.

Jem is my best pet.
I'm sad for Jem.
"This isn't like Jem,"
I said.

"Let's get to the vet," I said.
I led Jem to a nice vet.
"If Jem is sick,
this vet can help."

That vet checked Jem.
"Jem isn't sick," she said.
"Jem is just sad.
Does Jem have friends?"

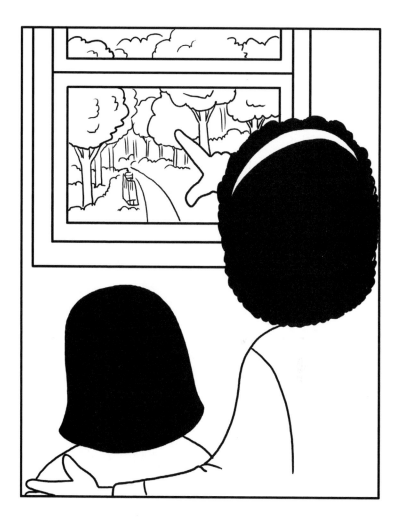

"It'll help if Jem spends
more time with pups," the vet said.
That vet had me
take Jem to the park.

Jem was full of life
at the park.
Jem ran with pups and had fun.
Now I'm not sad for Jem.

56

Herb Helps Out

Written by Shanna Marcus
Illustrated by Ken Furlie

Phonics Skills

R-controlled er, ir, ur				Syllables VCCV	
Herb's	bird	Herb	her	butter	batter
first	third	stir	stirred	better	after
shirt	stirring	turned		until	

Herb's mom was making
a cake shaped like a bird.
Herb was helping.
He liked making this cake.

Herb's mom needed butter
for her cake.
She asked Herb to get it for her.
Herb got his bench first.

Herb had to stand on his bench.
He saw butter in the third box.
Herb got the butter for Mom.

Herb's mom put milk and
eggs in the batter.
Herb helped get those things too.

Herb helped stir the batter.
At first Herb stirred fast,
but he got spots on his shirt.
Herb got better at stirring.
He did not stir fast after that.

Herb's mom put the batter
in her bird pan.
She turned her clock.
It would take until five.

When the cake was done,
Herb and Mom made it into a bird.
It made Herb's dad smile.

Fletch and Fran

Written by Tina Johannsen
Illustrated by Dan Vick

Phonics Skill

Plurals -s, -es

places	things	lots	lunches	berries
notes	bases	stands	tunes	classes
puppies	races	crafts		

Fletch and Fran are friends.
They do things together.
Fletch and Fran go places
and see lots of things.

At lunchtime, Fletch and Fran
trade sack lunches.
Fran's dad packs berries.
Fletch likes berries.

Fran and Fletch give nice notes.
Fran hopes Fletch does well on his test
Fletch tells her about a fun plan he ha

Fletch hit a home run.
Fran is glad.
When Fletch runs bases,
Fran likes to sit in the stands
and yell for him.

Fran got a prize for singing.
When Fran sings tunes,
Fletch won't miss it.
He thinks her singing is nice.

Fletch's mom drives them
home after classes.
They do work for class.
Then they spend time in the park.

Fletch and Fran run with
puppies at the park.
They run races
and make crafts.
Fletch and Fran have fun.

Bert Does Not Like Bugs

Written by Julie Walsh
Illustrated by Carmen Billings

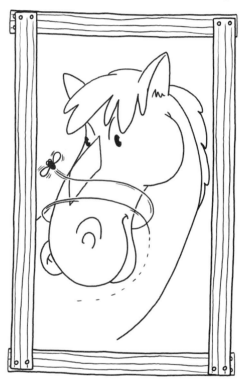

Phonics Skills

Long a: a, ai, ay				Syllables VCV
main	days	stay	tail	away
play	away	brain	pail	visit
raises	waits			

Bert is a nice horse.
But Bert does not like bugs.
Bert's main problem is
that bugs like Bert.

74

On hot days, bugs visit Bert's barn.
Bugs get on Bert's back.
Bert yells, "Scram!"
but the bugs stay.

Bert swishes his tail.
Those bugs think Bert
wants to play with them.
That will not make them go away.

Bert is getting upset.
He uses his brain
to come up with a plan.

Bert fills a big pail.
He raises it up.
Then Bert waits for the bugs.

Bert raises his tail.
He swings it hard at the pail.
Splash! Bert got a nice bath,
and those bugs got wet.

Now the bugs stay away.
That's how Bert likes it.

Our Reading Party

Written by Melissa Stevens
Illustrated by Bob Atkinson

Phonics Skills

Long e: e, ee, ea, y				Syllables VCV
reading	read	we	week	easy
party	teacher	each	please	Dena
clean	need	team	be	Steven
easy	sweeping	Dee	Danny	Peter
Dena	cleaning	Steven	Jean	even
Lee	Peter	seats	feel	
readers	treat	sweet	cream	
even				

The kids in my class like reading.
We read and read.
In fact, we got a prize
for reading a lot.

This week we are having
a big party.
Our teacher gave
each kid a job.

"Please clean up this room,"
our teacher said.
"We need to clean as a team.
It will be easy that way."

Dee is sweeping.
Danny is picking things up.
Dena is cleaning the glass.
Steven is dusting that shelf.

We bring things for this party.
Jean is bringing cups.
Lee is bringing plates.
Mike is bringing napkins.
Peter is bringing forks.

86

We sat in our seats.
"You must feel good!"
our teacher said.
"You are good readers.
This prize is such a nice treat."

We clapped.
Then we had cake and sweet ice cream.
Our party was a blast!
We will read even more to win again.

Sam's Stroll

Written by Julia Jameson
Illustrated by Pam Flarity

Phonics Skills

Long o: o, oa, ow				Syllables VCV
old	most	gold	go	favor
so	slow	stroll	road	robot
boat	toad	hello	row	open
over	croaked	bold	robot	
floated	cold	goat	no	
told	open	strolled		

Sam is an old farm cat.
He sits on his porch most days.
Every day is the same.
Sam likes it that way.

But on this day Sam feels different.
The grass is green.
The sun is gold.
The soft wind is nice.

"It is time for me
to go," Sam said.
And so he did.
Sam went for a slow stroll
on the dirt road.

92

Sam saw a boat
with three mice and a toad.
"Hello!" yelled Sam.
"Can you row me over there
as a favor?"

"Yes, we can,"
croaked that bold toad like a robot.
Sam floated across
the cold pond in that boat.

Sam hopped out.
An old goat was at the gate.
"May I open this gate?" Sam asked.
"No, I will do it,"
the goat told Sam.

That goat pushed it open.
Sam sat for a while
with the nice goat.
Then he strolled home.

Bill's Happy Day

Written by Molly Pizziferro
Illustrated by Michelle Olenick

Phonics Skill
Compound Words

driveway	backyard	bedroom	riverbank
weekend	cannot	birthday	teardrop
mailbox	mailman	mailbag	

June visited Bill's home.
Bill is not in his driveway.
He is not in his backyard.
He is not in his bedroom.
Where is Bill?

June went to the river.
Bill was sitting
on the riverbank.
He seemed sad.

"Hello, Bill!" June said.
"Put on a smile!
It's such a nice weekend.
You cannot be sad
on a day like this!"

100

"This is my birthday," Bill said.
"I didn't even get a card."
A teardrop rolled
off his cheek.

"Have you checked?"
June asked.
"No," Bill said.
"Then how can you tell
that you got no mail?" June asked.

Bill and June went
to Bill's mailbox.
Bill had no mail waiting for him.
He turned to go back in his house.

"Wait," June yelled. "I see someone.
That mailman is running late.
He has something big in his mailbag!"
His bag is stuffed with cards and gifts
for Bill!

Rose Flies Home

Written by Kyle Hickey
Illustrated by Kerry Buckner

Phonics Skills

Long i: i, ie, igh, y				Syllables VCV
bright	sky	I	try	spider(s)
spider(s)	fright	cry	tiny	tiny
finds	my	child	flight	
fly	high	I'll	sight	
I'm	flying	cries		

It is a bright day.
The sunny sky is fine.
"I must try to get home on time,"
Rose said.

Rose sees a spider
on the sidewalk.
It gave her a fright,
but she won't cry.

"Some spiders bite," she said,
"but this tiny spider is nice."
That spider strolls off.
Rose went on.

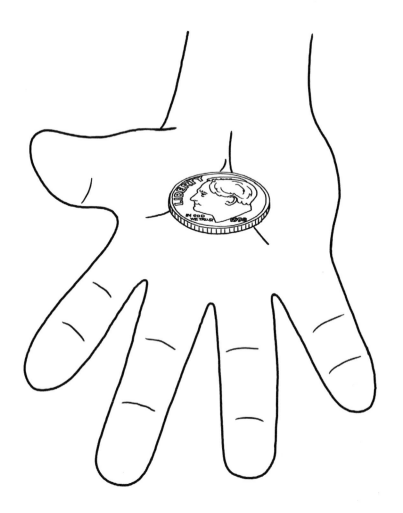

Rose finds a dime.
"For my bank," she said,
picking it up.
"I will save it for a treat."
The child went on her way.

Rose sees a plane in flight.
"Planes fly fast
and very high," she said.
"They must land on time."

110

Then Rose jumped and ran.
"Mom told me to be home
on time," she said.
"I'll run right home."

Her home is in sight.
Rose acts like a plane
in the sky.
"I'm flying home!" she cries.
She lands right on time.

112

A Day in the City

Written by Steven Kaye
Illustrated by Elizabeth Wimmer

Phonics Skill
Comparative Endings -er, -est

faster	tighter	nicer	higher	saddest
happier	harder	colder	brightest	brighter
longer	happiest			

Kelly visited a big city.
"Cars go faster in this city
than at home," Mom said.

"People go much faster, too,"
Dad added as he stepped
out of a man's way.
Kelly held tighter
to Mom's hand.

They went to a store.
"This is a nice scarf," Kelly said.
"It's nicer than my old scarf."
"These prices are higher,"
Mom added.
116

They went to a park.
"That is the saddest duck,"
Kelly said.
"He would be happier
at our pond."

The wind started blowing harder.
"It's getting colder," Mom noted.
"We must go inside."
They went to a shop
that sold hot drinks.

After dark, the street lit up.
"Those are the brightest lights
I've ever seen!" Kelly said.
"It is brighter than day!"

"We cannot stay longer,"
Dad told them.
Kelly was glad.
"I like this city," she said,
"but I'm happiest at home."